THE UNITED STATES LIFE-SAVING SERVICE — 1880

THE MORNING ROUND.

SURFMAN'S SHIELD.

THE UNITED STATES LIFE-SAVING SERVICE — 1880
by J.H. Merryman*

THE PATROL.

*James H. Merryman, according to <u>Harper's Magazine</u> (1882), as an officer of the revenue marine, was chief inspector of the board examining the crews of the life-saving stations.

A WRECK ON BARNEGAT SHOALS.

DRAWN BY W. TABER.

ENGRAVED BY C. W. CHADWICK.

A DISTRESSED SHIP.

Wreck of the Steamer _METROPOLIS_ on Currituck Beach, January 1878, with 85 lives lost.

The patrol had passed the point where the wreck occurred some two hours before. Peculiar cries, like that of many human voices mingled with the shrieks of the sea, led to the discovery of the stranded vessel by persons on the shore, who could see nothing through the fog. A boy was sent running to the nearest house, half a mile inland, the occupant of which mounted his horse and galloped to the nearest station, some four and a half miles away. The mortar cart, with apparatus, a dead-weight of more than a thousand pounds, was hauled through the wet, yielding sand, into which the wheels cut four or five inches, as fast as six strong, willing surfmen could hurry along. They were overtaken within a mile and a half of the scene by a man with a horse and cart — one of the features of the North Carolina beach — who, finding them worn down with their burden, hitched on and helped them through.

Three or four precious hours had already been consumed; the water was filled with floating fragments of the wreck. Efforts to throw the shot-line failed, and the despairing people, giving up all hope of rescue before the ship should break entirely in pieces, accepted their last alternative, plunging into the treacherous waves. The surf was running high, and the struggling, drowning mass of human beings drifted toward the shore. The life-savers and citizens ran into the water to meet and save them, and strove nobly in the inner breakers and undertow, dragging them ashore in great numbers. The incidents of that awful hour defy any attempts at description. The air was filled with encouraging shouts and agonizing screams. Upward of a hundred were rescued, and many were restored from apparent death. A handsome Newfoundland dog partic-piated in the work, incited by the example of his master, and came dripping through the surf, bringing safely ashore a half-drowned man.

Harper's Monthly, February 1882.

FRAGMENTS OF WRECKS ON THE BEACH.

DRAWN BY CARLTON T. CHAPMAN.   ENGRAVED BY H. E. SYLVESTER.

LAUNCH OF THE SURF-BOAT, JUPITER LIFE-SAVING STATION.

BOAT IN SAND-DRIFT.

STATION-HOUSE AT BARNEGAT.

THE UNITED STATES LIFE-SAVING SERVICE—1880

EDITOR'S PREFACE

The United States Life-Saving Service was at its heyday in 1880 when author Merryman had this article published in *Scribner's Monthly*, a national periodical of that early day. Shipping had been growing on the coasts of the nation—especially along the Atlantic shore—and so had the number of shipwrecks, with the consequent loss of life and property.

The need for a life-saving service had been recognized as early as 1848, but it wasn't until 1871 when the few rude huts already established were organized into a coherent system. Soon the Service flourished. The good it did was obvious to all. In a way the Life-Saving Service was a back-up system designed to step forward when the light-house warning system failed. A light might not be visible through the fog or storm-clouds. A ship's pilot might mistake one light for another and head into a shoal instead of around it. A lightship, stationed offshore, might drift off course. A ship might lose its steering. A fire might beak out aboard. Any of these mishaps—and others as well—not only might happen, but they did happen. When they happened during a storm, actually a likely time for something to go wrong, the ship was instantly in severe trouble, and often disaster soon followed.

Typically, a ship in distress would either be driven toward shore before the storm or would deliberately take a course for there to avoid sinking in deep water far offshore. At least there would be the hope of launching lifeboats or climbing into the rigging of the masts after the boat's bottom struck the sand and sank in shallow water. But launching a lifeboat safely from a listing wreck and then guiding the small craft through rolling breakers barricading the shore was a feat in itself. Surviving a freezing night clinging to broken masts above a deck washed by whitecaps was another. Yes, rescue from shore was the logical answer.

NAG'S HEAD—SCENE OF THE "HURON" DISASTER.

But the men on shore faced much the same risks in getting out to the ships. Too, there were often broken timbers and casks tossing in the surf. Nevertheless, their ingenuity, training, skill, equipment inventions, dependable surveillance, and daring heroism saved many a life—with the loss of some of their own number unfortunately. The methods the live-savers used, along with their cool dedication, is the emphasis in this article. The illustrations enhance the inherent drama of the situations, and most accompanied the original appearance; others have been added from contemporary sources, as: *Harper's Monthly* (1851, '66, '69, '71, '78), *Scribner's Magazine* (1888, 1891), *Century Magazine* (1889 and 1902), and *The Memorial Story of America* (1892).

Here, then, is good nostalgic history written close to the time when it happened, and of an important American institution of the day. It gives an idea, too, of the beginnings of the U.S. Coast Guard, created in 1915 by the consolidation of the Revenue-cutter Service and the Life-Saving Service of the Treasury Department, and now dedicated to much the same functions as this Life-Saving Service predecessor. Of course there are fewer shipwrecks today. Electronic wizardry and the mechanization of the sea have solved many former problems and even rendered rescue itself more efficient.

Although in part redundant of some of the points of the main article, we have appended another early (1851) account from *Harper's Magazine:* "Some Account of Francis's Life-boats and Life-cars" by Jacob Abbott. This includes mechanical details of metal vessels and also stories of harrowing rescue for both good history and exciting reading.

Reading these stories will give a better understanding and appreciation of this part of the American heritage, a story especially intriguing if one happens to be at the site of one of the early life-saving stations and watching a reenactment showing how the apparatus was used and the rescues made. Several such stations are now preserved in national park areas such as Cape Lookout and Cape Hatteras National Seashores. Beach apparatus drills have been presented at Sandy Hook and Island Beach (New Jersey), Cape Hatteras (North Carolina), and Golden Gate (California). If you are so fortunate as to witness one of these demonstrations, remember that when the men of the Life-Saving Service did their "demonstrations" a century and more ago that it was just as likely to be at night, in storm surf, with hurricane winds, and at sub-freezing

LIFE-SAVING STATION ON THE NORTH CAROLINA BEACH.

temperatures. John Krisko, National Park Service Chief Interpreter at Sandy Hook, reports a season's presentation of the Beach Apparatus Drill as follows:

"It took us 20 minutes to do the drill on a still, hot summer day as compared with six minutes during its heyday. Hauling the beach cart through 500 feet of loose sand was about my endurance limit. I am 50 now, but proved more durable than some of the younger guys. Executing the drill increases admiration of, and appreciation for, the brave men of the Life Saving Service. Many were older than I, but weathered many a Nor'easter and perilous ride through the surf."

William R. Jones
Series Editor

6

"Against its growing flush the cold waves rose and fell, and with them the boat and the two benumbed men."

UNITED STATES LIFE-SAVING STATION ON THE EASTERN COAST.

THE UNITED STATES LIFE-SAVING SERVICE—1880

by J. H. Merryman

In the principal newspapers of commercial cities there may be seen, under the caption of "Marine Intelligence," or some such title, a column made up of items, set in nonpareil type, like the following, cut from a recent journal:

Bark Halcyon (of Bath) Dickinson, from Boston for Perth Amboy, in ballast, went ashore on Long Beach, LI, AM of Sept 4. All hands were taken off by the crew of Life-Saving Station No. 32.

Has the reader any idea of the stirring drama a dry paragraph like this may conceal? Let us endeavor to make it apparent.

No portion of the ten thousand and more miles of the sea and lake coast-line of the United States, extending through every variety of climate and containing every feature of coast danger to the mariner, can exhibit a more terrible record of shipwreck than the long stretch of sandy beaches lying between Cape Cod and Cape Hatteras. Of this region the New Jersey coast is notoriously the worst. It has been said that if all the skeletons of vessels lying upon or imbedded in the sand between Sandy Hook and Barnegat could be ranged in line, the ghastly array would reach from one point to the other. Here, in 1848, the government placed a few rude huts that formed the nucleus from which the United States Life-Saving Service has been developed. These were intended to afford shelter to distressed mariners and to contain boats and such other life-saving appliances as were then known, volunteers from among the fishermen being relied upon to use them on occasions of shipwreck. And right gallantly, in many instances, did the brave beachmen respond, though their undertakings and deeds remain mostly unwritten, existing chiefly in the legends of the coast. Congress continued small appropriations from time to time, until Long Island was also provided with huts and a small increase was made to the number on the coast of New Jersey. But from lack of proper direction and want of system the movement languished and subsided. In the meantime, the Royal National Life-boat Institution, a society started in Great Britain under royal patronage nearly forty years prior to our own attempt, had gone on improving its methods and extending its means, and the people of other maritime nations were developing similar humane projects. The hour and the man at length came for our own institution. In 1871, Mr. Sumner I. Kimball, the present able General Superintendent, effected the organization of the service and introduced the existing system.

There are now upon the sea and lake coasts nearly two hundred life-saving stations, the greater number being established at the more dangerous and exposed points. The buildings are plain, yet picturesque,

cannot be launched from a flat beach on account of its great weight and huge size, objections which are unavoidable in securing the valuable qualities that distinguish it.

The main building has, below, a boat-room and a mess-room, or kitchen, each provided with convenient closets and lockers, and, above, two sleeping apartments and a store-room. The boat-room contains the surf-boat, which is used on flat beaches and in shoal waters. It is mounted on a light carriage, which may be drawn by the crew when draught animals are not available, unfortunately too often the case on remote outlying beaches. Within the same room also stands the mortar-cart loaded with the wreck ordnance, lines, and various implements, while properly bestowed throughout the apartment are various articles, most of which will come under our notice in the operations to be described. The kitchen and sleeping-rooms are sparingly provided with appropriate furniture, while the store-room is used for the stowage of the season's provisions, cordage, spare oars, etc. Here the keeper and crew live during the active season, which varies according to the latitude of the districts into which the coast is divided.

The keeper commands the crew of six surfmen. His position is one of grave responsibility, demanding long experience in his vocation and rare judgment in the execution of his important trusts. The selection

LIFE-SAVING STATION.

SELF-RIGHTING BOAT ON WAYS.

and similar in general dimensions and arrangement, though varying somewhat in outward design, according to location—those near cities or popular watering-places being in keeping with their surroundings and presenting a more finished appearance than those on desolate beaches. Those located in harbors or at inlets are each provided with an annex containing a self-righting and self-bailing life-boat, which

of his men, upon whose fidelity and skill depend not only his success, but oftentimes his life, as well as the fate of those whom he is expected to succor, is very properly confided solely to him. Both keeper and men are chosen from among the fishermen in the vicinity of the stations, who are most distinguished for their ability as surfmen. Draw-

DRILL AND EXERCISE IN THE SURF-BOAT.

ing their first breath within sound of the surf, they pass through childhood viewing the sea in all its moods. In early youth they make their first essay in the breakers, and from that on to manhood advance from the least important oar through regular gradations, until the most skillful reach the command of the boat. This life gives them familiarity with the portion of the beach upon which they dwell, and its bordering currents, eddies, and bars, and an intimate acquaintance with the habits of the surf. It is an erroneous notion that the experience of the sailor qualifies him for a surfboatman. The sailor's home is at sea. He gives the land a wide berth, and is never at ease except with a good offing. He is rarely called upon to ply an oar in a small boat, particularly in a high surf, and his vocation gives him little knowledge of the surfman's realm, which is the beach and a portion of the sea extending but little beyond the breakers. The number of mariners who are annually lost in attempting to land from stranded vessels through the surf in their own boats, sorrowfully attests this fact. On the other hand, the most expert surfman may not be, and often is not, a sailor, though generally he has an excellent knowledge of every part of a ship and her apparel, gained in his occupation of stripping wrecks.

The training of the surfmen as life-saving men is completed by officers of the Revenue Marine, whose own professional training, familiarity with the coast (acquired in their cruises along shore for the prevention of smuggling), and experience in assisting vessels in distress, especially qualify them for the duty.

The life of the station surfmen is rather a monotonous, though not an idle, one. Each day has its portion of drill and exercise in the various methods employed in rendering aid to the shipwrecked, and considerable of the spare time of the men is occupied in keeping the building and apparatus in repair, and in making improvements around the station. At night their duties become severe and often perilous. The interval from sunset to sunrise is divided into three watches. At the beginning of each watch two men set out from the station on patrol duty and follow their beats to the right and left respectively until they meet the patrolmen from the adjacent stations, with whom they exchange certain tokens as proof to the keepers in the morning of the faithful performance of the duty. The relieving watches keep up this scrutiny until sunrise, and, if the weather be foul, throughout the day. The meeting and exchange of tokens is required, of course, only upon continuous beaches, or uninterrupted stretches of coast, where the stations average a distance of from three to five miles apart. At isolated stations the limits of the patrol are fixed by specific boundaries. This watching of the beach is of cardinal importance, and neglect of the duty is punished by banishment from the service and prohibition of future employment.

The beach guardians are no idle promenaders. A march of four or five miles through the soft sea-sand is a task at any time; what is it in the fury of a winter storm? The prevalent strong winds, which must be encountered in one direction or the other of the beat, drive before them rain, snow, hail, and sleet, or oftener sharp sand, which cuts the face until, smarting with pain, the patrolman turns and walks backward for relief. Such is the force of this natural sand-blast that it soon dulls the glass of the patrol lanterns, and at some of the more exposed stations has made ground-glass of the window-panes. In a snow-storm the ocean beach is the wildest of pathless deserts, and even by daylight, shut out from prominent landmarks, the foam of the breaking surf alone serves to guide the panting patrolman on his way. Leaving it, he would wander helplessly among the sand-dunes that crown the beach. When the darkness of night is added, and his lantern, if not extinguished by the gale, but feebly lights his path through the slush of snow and sand, he strays and stumbles into pitfalls and quick-sands, to recover his way and accomplish his journey only through his life-long acquaintance with every foot of the ground. Sometimes, failing in this, benumbed with cold and bewil-

dered by his mishaps, he is found by his comrades in the snow insensible, or perhaps dead. Then there come, fortunately not often, the blast of the hurricane and the inundation of the tidal wave, pregnant with terrors indescribable. These are the tornadoes which, inland, uproot trees, unroof and prostrate buildings, destroy flocks and herds, and create general havoc. On the beach the stations are sometimes torn from their strong foundation-posts and overset and borne away by the flood, the inmates escaping as best they can. The patrolman cannot stand up against the fury. Again and again he is overthrown as he struggles to reach the top of a sand-hill, his only refuge from the waters which rush upon the land and sweep through the depressions between the hillocks, separating them into islets. In the memorable tempest of October 22 and 23, 1878, the patrolmen suffered severely, and several were in extreme peril. In one instance, a patrolman not returning in the morning, and his fellows not being able to discover him with their glasses from the look-out of the station, a boat expedition was sent in search of him among the still flooded sand-hills, upon one of which, nearly covered with water, he was at length found, barely alive.

When a vessel is driven ashore in a storm, the patrolman, being the first to discover her, takes the initiative steps in the operations for the rescue. He carries at night, besides his lantern, a signal, which ignited by percussion emits a red flame. He is quick to

LAUNCHING THE SURF-BOAT.

observe the slightest indication of a disaster: the glimmer of a light, the white apparition of a sail, the faint outline of a slender spar just beyond the breakers, or at his feet on the strand perhaps a grating, a bucket, or mile or two away. His hasty entrance is sufficient to arouse the slumbering inmates. Struggling for breath he makes his report, the nature of which determines to the keeper the means to be employed for the

THE NIGHT PATROL.

some other article which he knows to have come from a ship. Then with all his faculties bent to the search, he descries a vessel either too close in for safety or actually stranded in the breakers. In either case he burns his signal, whose crimson light flashes far out to sea, and warns the unwary ship to stand off, or assures the shipwrecked that aid is near at hand. Being certain it is a wreck, he hurries to his station, perhaps a rescue. If the surf-boat is to be taken, at the word of command the wide doors of the boat-room are thrown open and the boat-carriage drawn by willing hands rolls out, bearing the graceful craft fully equipped for service. In the absence of horses, the burden must be hauled by the men, and their laborious task may be conceived, when it is stated that each man must drag nearly one hundred and eighty pounds through soft, yielding sand, whatever the distance may be between the station and the wreck, while one hundred and fifty pounds is the estimated load for a man to draw over a level turnpike.

Arrived at the scene of the disaster, the boat is launched with as little delay as possible from a point opposite the wreck, in order to get the benefit of the slight breakwater which the position of the vessel affords, and is soon off and away on its errand of mercy. The height of human skill is required of the keeper standing at the steering oar to guide the boat safely in its passage through the wild running breakers. The surfmen, with their backs to the dangers lurking in the treacherous seas, do not go blindly to uncertain fate, for they rest their eyes continually upon the keeper, while they ply their oars in obedience to his commands, and mark his slightest gesture. Their first attempt is not always successful. Despite every care, a suddenly leaping sea may break, and fill the boat, compelling a return to the shore, or capsize her, tumbling the men into the water, where they are tossed about in the surf, but are sustained by their cork life-belts until making a foothold they struggle to the beach and righting the boat try again and perhaps a third or fourth time, before finally reaching the wreck. Here the most careful maneuvering is necessary to prevent collision of their light craft against the huge hull of the stranded vessel, or to avoid fatal injury from falling spars and floating wreckage. Taking off as best they can the anxious people, whom the overwhelming seas have driven into the rigging of the vessel, perhaps fast going to pieces, the difficult return to the shore remains before them. The keeper must now decide upon one of several methods of landing, as the nature of the sea may demand. Under favorable conditions he may run in immediately behind a roller, and by quick work keep well ahead of the following one, and so reach the beach in safety. With a different sea he may back in, occasionally pulling ahead to meet an incoming breaker; and again, for a worse sea he may use a drag to check the headway with which a swift rolling comber would otherwise carry the boat high upon its summit until a portion of the keel would be out of water, the bow high in the air and the stern still resting upon the crest,—from which position, on account of the slight hold the boat has in the water, the sea behind is liable, in spite of the efforts of the steersman, to turn it to the right or left, causing it to

" broach to " and capsize, or if this be avoided, perhaps to be " pitch-poled," end over end.

When the patrolman has reported at the station that the boat cannot be used, the mortar-cart is ordered out. Like the boat-carriage it must be drawn by the men, and though the load is somewhat lighter, the state of the sea or the weather increases the labor; the one compelling them to take a route close to the low sand-hills in the wash and foam of the spent breakers, or back of the hills in the looser sand by a circuitous course, and the other harassing and retarding them with its fury. Reaching at length their destination, each man, well trained in his duties, proceeds to handle and place in position the portion of the apparatus assigned to his special charge. Simultaneously the different members of the crew load the gun, place the shot-line box in position, dispose the hauling lines and hawser for running, attach the breeches-buoy, put the tackles in place ready for hauling, and with pick and spade begin the digging of a trench for the sand-anchor, while the beach lantern lights up the scene.

And now the gun is fired! The shot

BURNING A SIGNAL.

STRIPPING THE WRECK.

with its line goes flying against the gale, over the wreck into the sea beyond; the line falls across a friendly spar or rope, and is soon seized by the eager benumbed hands of the imperiled sailors, whose glad shouts, faintly heard on shore, make known to the life-savers their success. The surfmen connect the whip (an endless line), the tail-block and tally-board to the shot-line already being hauled in by the impatient sailors. The whip passes rapidly toward the wreck, and arriving there the sailors make fast the tail-block in accordance with the directions on the tally-board and show a signal to the shore. Hauling upon one part of the whip, the surfmen then send on board, attached to the other part, the hawser and a second tally-board, which directs how and where the end of the hawser should be secured to the wreck. The tackles now connecting the sand-anchor and the shore end of the hawser are hauled upon until the hawser is straight and taut, when it is lifted several feet in the air, and further tightened by the erection of a wooden crotch, which constitutes a temporary pier while the wreck answers for another, and the hawser stretched between the two suggests a suspension bridge in an early stage of construction with but

one cable in place. The breeches-buoy is drawn to and fro on the hawser, and by means of it the shipwrecked are brought safely to shore.

This method is expeditious when once well in operation, but is frequently attended with difficulties which evoke every resource and expedient. Often in storms a strong swift current runs along the coast between the outer bar and the shore, called by the surfmen the " set " or " cut," which, in connection with the action of the surf, twists and entangles the lines, as the attempt is made to haul them across from shore to ship, or sweeps them away to a great distance, causing heavy strains that sometimes prove too much for their strength. Occasionally, when the apparatus is well set up for use, the motion of the wreck, as it is lifted and rolled about by the powerful seas, is so violent and constant that, even with the most watchful care, the strong lines snap and break asunder like pack-thread; and at times the careless or bungling manner in which those on board perform their part, allowing the shot-line or the whip to saw across the stiff rigging of the vessel, or chafe against other portions of the wreck until it parts, hinders the work or altogether prevents success. Now and then, in extreme cold weather, the lines become rigid and clogged with ice as soon as they are exposed to the air when lifted out of the water; and again, unless proper care has been observed in the arrangement of the blocks and lines, the velocity with which the freighted ropes run through the blocks, may set on fire the wooden shells, or cases that contain the sheaves or pulley-wheels. These mishaps and reverses tax the patience and resources of the surfmen to the utmost, and often put their courage to the severest test. The breaking of the lines involves the toil and delay of the duplication of their work, and perhaps the anxious suspense necessitated by a return to the station for spare lines. Sometimes it is found necessary to abandon altogether the use of the hawser, and to draw the people ashore through the water with the whip and breeches-buoy, or even without the latter, the shipwrecked persons securing themselves into the whip by tying it around their bodies. In some of these contingencies people have been held suspended in the breakers or ensnarled in the floating cordage and *débris* of the vessel, and only extricated from their perilous positions by the most daring exploits of the surfmen who have worked themselves out through the surf, and, at the most imminent risk of their own lives, released the helpless beings from their bonds, or disentangled them by severing the meshes with their knives, and returned, bearing their gasping trophies safely to the shore.

Other accidents and obstacles are likely to embarrass the efforts of the life-saving crews, who usually arrive at the scene of disaster exhausted by their wearisome march.

The breeches-buoy, although it is an exceedingly useful contrivance for bringing men ashore, is hardly a suitable one for transporting women and children, or for rescuing a large number of persons with dispatch, or invalids whom it is necessary to protect from wet and exposure. In such cases the life-car is usually brought into requisition and used with the arrangement of ropes already described; or, as externally it is simply a covered boat, under favorable circumstances it may be drawn back and forth through the water by a line attached to each end. More frequently, however, it is connected with the hawser by a simple device, in such a manner as to permit it to float upon the water, while preventing it from drifting, in strong currents, too far from a direct course for the length of the hauling lines. The life-car is about two hundred

"A SHIP ASHORE!"

OFF TO A WRECK.

FIRING THE MORTAR.

pounds heavier than the breeches-buoy, and accordingly increases to that extent the burden of apparatus to be brought to the scene of a wreck; but it has sufficient capacity for five or six adults, and has carried, at a single trip, nine half-grown children. Practically water-tight, but provided with means for supplying air, its passengers are landed dry and without serious discomfort. The occasions of its use have been numerous, and in one notable instance —the wreck of the *Ayreshire* below Squan Beach, on the coast of New Jersey—two hundred and one persons were rescued by it, when no other means could have availed. Silks, fine fabrics, jewelry, and other valuable goods have often been saved by its use, and from one vessel the car took ashore a large sum in gold bullion belonging to the United States, together with the mails.

The general features of the Lake and Pacific coasts admit of the use of the self-righting and self-bailing life-boat. On the Lakes the stations are situated, with few exceptions, at, or very near, commercial towns, or cities having artificial harbors. These harbors are formed at the mouths of rivers by long piers projecting some distance into the lake. The passages between the piers are quite narrow and difficult to enter when high seas are running at right angles to them; thus vessels in attempting to go in are frequently thrown out of their course at the critical moment and are cast upon the end of a pier to quick destruction, or, escaping that danger, are driven ashore outside. Here the self-righting and self-bailing life-boat is used with good effect. This marvelous product of inventive thought, which has been developed by a century of study and experiment, from the first model, designed by the English coach-maker, Lionel Lukin, in 1780, is the best life-boat yet devised. It has great stability, and is with difficulty upset, but when this happens, it instantly rights itself, and when full of water empties itself in from fifteen to twenty seconds. The attainment of the first of these wonderful qualities is secured by means of a heavy iron keel, weighing from six hundred to fifteen hundred pounds, according to the size of the boat, and two large air-chambers placed in the bow and stern—the keel, when the boat is capsized, being drawn by the force of gravitation back toward and into the water, while the submerged air-chambers seek the surface at the same moment. The property of self-bailing is produced by the insertion of a deck or floor, some inches

above the load-line, in which there are placed several tubes extending down through the bottom of the boat, fitted with valves at the top, which open downward by the pressure of any water in the boat, and

SURFMAN WITH LIFE-BELT.

are self-closing when the pressure ceases. The draught and great weight which the construction of such a boat involves—the smallest weighs scarcely less than four thousand pounds—generally preclude its use, as has been stated, along the sandy flat beaches of the Atlantic. The Lake stations being inside the harbors and fronting directly upon or over comparatively smooth and sufficiently deep water, the heavy boats launched directly from their ways, are propelled by eight oars, or towed by a tug-boat out between the piers to the rescue. Not unfrequently, just before navigation is suspended by winter on the Lakes, a single life-saving crew is employed upon several vessels at a time. Recently four wrecks occupied half a station crew in the vicinity of their station on the same day, while the remainder were at work on a fifth, forty miles away, whither they had been transported by rail, on a special train secured for the occasion. It is a common occurrence for the life-boats to go under sail and oars ten or twelve miles from their stations to the

18

COAST PATROL.

assistance of vessels in distress. On the Pacific coast, where the prevailing gales blow along and not upon the shore, and where there are few outlying dangers, and these at long intervals apart, coast disasters are comparatively rare, and it has been deemed necessary to provide for the establishment of but eight stations. With one exception, these are at points where the self-righting and self-bailing life-boat is available.

But the work of the crews does not always end with the rescue. The pressing necessities of the moment administered to, the sufferers are led, supported, or carried, as their condition will admit, to the station, which is quickly transformed into a hospital. The neglected fire is replenished with fuel; the kitchen stove soon glows with heat; the plethoric clothes-bags and well-filled chests of the surfmen are opened, and dry clothing is put upon all that need it; snow and cold water, and afterward scrapings of raw potatoes from the mess stores, are applied to the frostbitten; the prostrated are put to bed in the extra cots provided in the upper rooms, and tenderly tucked in by rough hands, suddenly grown gentle; the medicine chest, filled with simple remedies and restoratives, is opened, and stimulants dispensed to the exhausted, while plasters, lint, and bandages are applied to those who have been bruised and wounded by the wreckage. Meanwhile,

shipwrecked and surfmen are inhaling the delicious aroma of boiling coffee, which the mess-cook deems it his first duty to prepare. This having been partaken of, the keeper designates the least weary of the crew to attend to the wants of the strangers, while the others retire for rest until required to relieve the watch.

Occasionally, in the exigencies of shipwreck, persons reach the shore senseless and seemingly without life. That the surfmen may be able to act intelligently in such cases, the regulations of the service contain plain directions for the application of a simple method for restoring the apparently drowned, in which the men are regularly practiced, according to the instructions of a medical officer of the Marine Hospital Service, who visits the stations once a year as a member of the board for the examination of the keepers and crews, as to their physical and professional qualifications. The principal features of the method are indicated by the cuts on page 27, one showing the first step taken, by which the chest is emptied of air, and the ejection of any fluids that may have been swallowed is assisted; and the other the position and action of the operator, in alternately producing artificial expiration and inspiration, in imitation of natural breathing, which may be expected to ensue if the patient is not really dead.

HAULING THE MORTAR CAR.

20

BREECHES-BUOY APPARATUS IN OPERATION. "HAUL AWAY!"

There are many appliances auxiliary to the principal means employed in the operations of the service, of which space will not permit present notice. The life-saving dress, however, which has been made familiar to the public through the exploits and expeditions of Paul Boyton, is one of considerable importance, and on several occasions has been used with great advantage. At the stranding of a schooner in the night on Lake Ontario last year, in a sea which would not admit of the use of the boat, a shot-line was fired over her, with the intention of setting up the lines for the use of the breeches-buoy. The sailors hauled the whip-line on board, and when the tally-board, on which the directions for the method of procedure are printed in English on one side and French on the other, was received, the captain attempted by the light of a lantern to read them. Puzzling over them for some time, he at length contemptuously threw the board down on the deck, finding it impossible to make anything of it, having seen only the French side.

Not knowing what else to do, therefore, he simply made the line fast, but in such a manner that it could not be worked from the shore. The surfmen vainly endeavored to convey instruction by signs. In the meantime, the destruction of the vessel and the loss of all on board seemed imminent. In this dilemma, one of the surfmen put on the life-saving dress, and, after a gallant struggle, succeeded in hauling himself along the line through the breakers to the vessel, where he remained and took charge of the operations on board until all were safely landed. On another occasion three sailors, in spite of the warning signals of the life-saving crew, committed the common error of attempting to land in one of the ship's boats. A strong current was running between the ship and the beach, and the water was full of porridge-ice for a long distance from the shore. Knowing what would happen, two of the surfmen put on their life-saving dresses and ran up the beach, with difficulty maintaining their race with the boat, which continued for

THE BREECHES BUOY.

from an outlying beach in his life-saving dress, had just crossed a wide slough, and rising suddenly among the reeds on its muddy banks, beheld two snipe shooters a hundred yards away, gazing in undisguised astonishment. " I seen they was mighty skeered," said he, " and took me for the devil or some other sea varmint, so I beginned to cut up and prance round like a yearlin' calf in a two-acre medder, a-yellin' and a-screechin' all the time as loud as I could holler, and ye'd jest orter seen them fellers scoot fur the cedars. I guess they's runnin' yit." To a doubting Thomas who asked, " But whar was their guns all this time ? " he replied : " Pshaw ! them fellers never knowed they had no guns." The hunters' version of the adventure has never reached the beach, but it may easily be imagined.

When the life-saving dresses were first introduced into the service, the surfmen regarded them with as little favor as they usually manifest for any innovation upon the simple devices and methods which were transmitted to them from their fathers, especially as regards appliances for their own safety, such as life-belts and cork jackets. They prefer to rely upon their skill and endurance as swimmers, with unencumbered limbs and bodies. Probably, also, a certain degree of pride disinclines them to wear anything that might suggest the least suspicion of a faint heart. For a long time, to insure their use in the face of these prejudices, firm and judicious measures on the part of the officers of the service were required, and the life-belts were not willingly donned by the men throughout the service until they had been taught a sad lesson, by the capsizing of a surf-boat and the loss of the crew, who had gone to a wreck at night without them. Only recently, a brave volunteer, on taking an oar in a station boat, in a dangerous sea on Cape Cod, was proffered a spare life-belt but declined it, saying : " Oh, no ! I don't want to go floating by Highland Light carrying a deck load of cork." The life-belt is manufactured from selected cork, and is so adjusted that the wearer has free use of his limbs in any position. Its buoyancy is sufficient to support two men in the water. Since its adoption by the men, none have been drowned, although many have been thrown into the water by capsized boats.

The life-saving men, of course, must have their hours of relaxation. Among the people of the coast, more than elsewhere,

the distance of two miles, until reaching an open space in the ice, the sailors attempted to land, when they were capsized in the surf, but were rescued from drowning by the surfmen, who rushed into the breakers and safely dragged them ashore.

Clad in the life-saving dress, the wearer presents a strange appearance, and to an uninitiated observer he might seem, while engaged in his weekly practice, to be some amphibious monster, disporting one moment in the water and the next on land. Sometimes in cold weather, a surfman thus arrayed, goes on some errand from the station to the mainland, his route being an air-line across deep sloughs or creeks and wet marshes for two or three miles. A surfman once going

22

perhaps, a pronounced religious sentiment prevails; hence, carousing and gaming and other immoralities are rarely indulged in. Especially is this true at the stations, where prohibitory regulations add their restraint. Each station is provided with a substantial library of well-selected books, the donations of generous people, with the view of contributing to the diversion of the crews and the solace of the victims of shipwreck who may be temporarily detained there. These libraries are the source of much entertainment and instruction to the men. In fine, clear weather, when the wind is off shore, and there is little occasion for anxiety, the surfmen gather in the mess-room and while away the time rehearsing the legends of the coast, spinning yarns, singing, or listening to the tuneful strains of violin or flute. Now and then, when the moon is full, there is a "surprise party" at the station. From the mainland or the neighboring settlements come men and women, the friends and relatives of the surfmen, bringing cakes and pastries, and other good things from their homes. Then all is joy unconfined; the boat-room is cleared of carriage and cart, and the merry dance goes round. Do not imagine, however, that in these festivi-

that, with wife or sweetheart to share his vigils, the patrolman yearns not for the pleasures at the station?

A mute but interested spectator of the entertainment is perhaps a Newfoundland dog. These noble animals, whose good qualities are so well known, are kept at many of the stations and they often seem instinctively to understand the object of the service, to which they soon become faithfully attached. The celebrated picture of Landseer, entitled "A Distinguished Member of the Humane Society," will readily be recalled by the reader. One remarkable illustration which the service furnishes of the characteristics of this sagacious animal is worthy of note. At the sad disaster to the steamship *Metropolis* on the coast of North Carolina, while the life-saving men were engaged in rescuing the crowd of passengers thrown into the sea by the breaking up of the vessel, a large Newfoundland dog belonging to a gentleman residing in the vicinity, seemed suddenly to comprehend the situation, and joining the throng of rescuers, plunged into the surf, seized a drowning man, and dragged him safely ashore. Shortly afterward he left his master and went to the station of the crew

THE SELF-RIGHTING LIFE-BOAT.

ties the patrol is relaxed. Not at all; the rule is inflexible, and its violation would be discovered. Indeed, who knows that the beach watch is not then doubled and

with whom he rendered this first service in life-saving, and there he still remains, steadily resisting every inducement to return to his former master. Every alternate night he sets out with one of the first patrol and accompanies him until the patrolman from the next station below is met, when he joins the latter and proceeds with him to that station, where he remains until the first watch of the next night, when he returns to his own station in the same manner. These self-assumed duties he performs with the peculiar gravity of demeanor that distinguishes his species, changing his station daily, for some good and sufficient dog-reason, no doubt, while very sensibly keeping but one watch each night.

The plan of the organization of the service is simple but effective. The coast-line is divided into twelve districts, there being eight on the Atlantic coast, three on the

marine, make stated inspections and drill the crews. The entire service is under the charge and management of a general superintendent, whose office is a bureau of the Treasury Department. All the officers of the service are invested with the powers of customs officers, which enable them to protect the interests of the government in preventing smuggling, and assisting in securing the collection of duties upon dutiable wrecked goods. They are also required to guard wrecked property until the owners or their agents appear.

The officers and men of the service are chosen without reference to any other consideration than those of professional fitness and integrity. In the introduction and

THE SELF-RIGHTING LIFE-BOAT UNDER SAIL.

Lakes, and one on the Pacific. In each of these the stations are distinguished by numbers, from one upward, beginning at the most northerly or easterly. Each district is under the immediate charge of a superintendent, who must be a resident thereof, and familiar with the character and peculiarities of its coast-line. He nominates the keepers of the stations, makes requisition for needed supplies, etc., and pays the crews their wages. To each district is also assigned an inspector, who is the commanding officer of the revenue cutter whose cruising grounds embrace the limits of the district. These officers, under the direction of a chief inspector, who is also an officer of the revenue

maintenance of this principle of selection much opposition and difficulty have been encountered. In the older districts, owing to the fact that until 1871 the keepers of stations were regarded only as custodians of public property, without responsibility in the success or failure of efforts at wrecks, surfmanship was not a standard of qualification, and these positions were generally made the rewards of political service by each of the parties, as they alternately succeeded to power; and so, when the employment of crews was authorized, the local politicians endeavored to control the appointment of these also. Their success soon became only too evident, and it was to

LIFE-BOAT

APRIL 19, 1884:

SAMBRO ISLAND, the scene of the late terrible wreck of the *Daniel Steinmann*, marks one of the most dangerous points along that iron-bound northeast coast where so many vessels have been driven to destruction. It is a small rocky ledge in the Atlantic Ocean almost covered by the waves in stormy weather. On it is a lighthouse, a white octagonal tower, showing a fixed light 115 feet above the sea at high water, and visible twenty-one miles in clear weather. It is about a mile and a half from the shore at Cape Sambro, and bears from Chedabuctoo Head, the western point of entrance to Halifax Harbor, southwest four and one-third miles. In foggy weather vessels are warned by heavy guns on the island of their approach to the dangerous ledges around it. Of these ledges the Sisters are the most dangerous. Several of them are bare at low water. The lead gives little or no warning when approaching these ledges

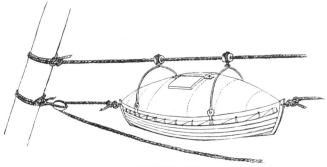

LIFE-SAVING CAR.

STATION.

from the eastward, there being forty-five fathoms of water within less than half a mile from the Sisters. Sambro Island is the resort of pilots. Halifax Harbor, where the *Daniel Steinmann* was bound, is one of the finest in the world, but the dangers of its entrance require the greatest care. The fogs at this season of the year are dense. The unfortunate vessel was but two or three hundred yards from the light when she struck the ledge that knocked a great hole in her bottom, and caused over 100 souls to be engulfed almost without warning. The Nova Scotia authorities are censured because the Sambro lighthouse was provided with neither boat nor life-saving apparatus. Had these been at hand, it is believed that the list of the rescued would be much greater than nine out of 136.

—Frank Leslie's Illus. Newspaper

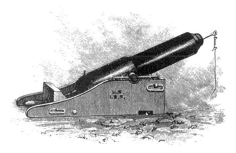

THE LYLE GUN.

counteract these injurious influences that the board of examination already mentioned was constituted. A thorough inspection of the service was made; every station was visited, the incompetent were dismissed, and qualified men were employed in their places. These advantageous changes in the corps somewhat altered its political complexion, and the nullification of the effort to subordinate the service to political ends was not quietly accepted. Threats and appeals were in turn resorted to, to overcome the determination of those in charge of the service. Upon the establishment of new districts, similar attempts to gain control of them are generally made, but they are not so tenaciously persisted in. These attempts are not confined to the party in power. No sooner is a keeper appointed from the opposition than he is beset with solicitations and demands to remember his party friends. The official injunction, however, issued yearly, at the commencement of the season, to the superintendents and keepers, that only capability and worth are to be regarded in the choice of their subordinates, supplemented by the action of the examining board, keeps the service well exempt from political domination.

But, it will be asked, what results have been attained by the service? At this writing, the last published report is that of the fiscal year ending June 30th, 1878. From this it appears

TALLY-BOARD AND WHIP-BLOCK.

that during that year there were 171 disasters to vessels within the limits of the operations of the service. There were on board these vessels 1,557 persons. The number of lives saved was 1,331, the number lost 226, and the number of days' succor afforded to shipwrecked persons at the stations was 849. Of the 226 lost, 183 perished at the disasters to the steamers *Huron* and *Metropolis*, the former occurring four days prior to the manning of the stations, which the appropriations for the maintenance of the service did not then permit to take place until the first of December, and the latter occurring at a distance so remote from the nearest station as to render prompt aid impossible;—defects which the reports of the service had repeatedly pointed out, and asked to have remedied. The loss of fourteen others occurred where service was impeded by distance, or where the stations were not open. Making allowance for these, the loss of life legitimately within the scope of life-saving operations, was twenty-nine.

LIFE-SAVING DRESS.

The sad catastrophes of the *Huron* and *Metropolis* contributed largely in securing the passage of the effective bill of June, 1878, which was introduced and warmly advocated by Hon. S. S. Cox, and which number of persons on board the vessels involved was 6,287; the number saved was 5,981; the number lost 306,† and the number of days relief afforded to shipwrecked persons at the stations, 3,716.

RESUSCITATION: EJECTING WATER FROM BODY.

established the service on a stable basis, with powers and functions somewhat commensurate with its purposes and capabilities.* From November, 1871, the date of the inauguration of the present system, to It should be observed that during the first of these seven years the service was limited to the coasts of Long Island and New Jersey; the two following years, to those coasts, with the addition of Cape Cod;

RESUSCITATION: RESTORING RESPIRATION.

the 30th of June, 1878, the number of disasters stated to have occurred within the field of operations of the service was 578; the the next year. to the foregoing, with the addition of the coasts of New England and the coast from Cape Henry to Cape Hatteras; the next, to the foregoing, with the ad-

* In this connection, acknowledgments are also due to the Hon. Charles B. Roberts, who made an exhaustive report upon the subject from the Committee on Commerce, seconded by an extremely able speech. The measure was also warmly supported by the Hon. Messrs. Covert, Conger, Yeates, Crapo, Dunnell, Brogden, Pugh, and others. In previous years the service was also much indebted to Senators Stockton, Hamlin, Boutwell, Chandler and Frelinghuysen, and to Representatives Newell, Haight, Lynch, Hale of Maine, Hooper, Cox and Conger.

† This number includes the 183 persons who perished at the wrecks of the *Huron* and *Metropolis* and the 14 others above referred to.

dition of the coast from Cape Henlopen to Cape Charles; the next, to all the foregoing, with the addition of Florida and the lake coasts; and the last year, to the coast at present included.

It is not claimed that the entire number of persons designated in the above figures as saved would have perished but for the aid of the life-saving crews, since not unfrequently, in cases of shipwreck by stranding, a portion of the imperiled succeed in escaping to the shore, as did several in the instance of the *Huron;* and it often happens that the sudden subsidence of the sea spares the threatened vessels from destruction. But it is certain that a large proportion of the number would have perished. A closer approximation to the real efficacy of the service could be reached, if statistics of the loss of life in former years upon the coasts where life-saving stations are now established could be obtained. Unfortunately no such record exists, except an imperfect one, consisting of meager data relative to disasters between 1850 and 1870 in the vicinity of the rude station-huts of the Long Island and New Jersey coasts. It is known that this record by no means includes near all the disasters which occurred on these coasts. A comparison, however, of the record of the service since

MEDICINE CHEST, LANTERNS, ETC.

1871 with this list shows an average annual reduction in the loss of life of about 87 per cent!

The record is a shining one. How much of it is due to official organization may readily be conceived, but it is less easy to realize how much of it belongs to the gallant crews of the stations, some of whose hardships, together with the methods they employ, the foregoing pages disclose. The professional skill of these men, their unfaltering energy and endurance, their steady bravery in the hour of supreme ordeal, and at all times their sober fidelity to duty, however

THE MESS-ROOM, "WHEN THE WIND IS OFF SHORE."

THE LIFF-OAR IN ACTION.

hard or irksome, are beyond all tribute. None can better know it than the officers in charge of the service, whose main reliance must be, after all, upon the manly virtue of these crews. What, indeed, can ever stand in lieu of men!

Many things are yet needed in aid of the labors of the crews. Numerous articles of outfit and equipment are required, which the appropriations, so far, have not been sufficient to provide; an imperative need is an additional man for each station; at present, when a wreck occurs, the station is left without a proper custodian, who would thus be provided to guard the public property and to keep the house in the state of comfortable preparation befitting the return from a rescue of the exhausted crew, with a convoy of drenched, frozen, wounded, and famished people. In the routine of station duty, another man would also greatly relieve the others, now too severely tasked. Another urgent requirement at many of the stations is horses, which Congress should provide. The heavy draught labors involved in hauling a ponderous load of apparatus for miles to a wreck would thus be spared the men, giving them time and

THE STORM SIGNAL.

strength for their daring and perilous work of rescue. Another need, surely, is pensions for those who are permanently disabled in the line of their duty, and for the widows and orphans of those who perish in the endeavor to save life from shipwreck. The guns trained to destroy life in the service of the country carry this grateful condition. The guns trained to save life, no less in the service of the country, have an equal right to carry it also. What soldiers have a better claim to this form of public remembrance than the noble beachmen who surrender life, as did those in North Carolina, in 1876, when endeavoring to rescue the sailors of the *Nuova Ottavia* ?

In the thought of this deed let us close. A gallant soul whose name honors the rolls of the Life-Saving Service, once said: " When I see a man clinging to a wreck, I see nothing else in the world, and I never think of family and friends until I have saved him." It is certain that this is the spirit which pervades the men of the coast. All report, all record testifies to it, and every winter their deeds sublimely respond to the divine declaration : " Greater love hath no man than this, that a man lay down his life for his friends."

WRECK OF THE SCHOONER "HARTZEL" IN LAKE MICHIGAN.

"Longest of all was the time before the boat came back."

PATROLMEN EXCHANGING CHECKS.

The following article is reprinted from *Harper's Magazine*, 1851.

THE LIFE-CAR.

SOME ACCOUNT OF FRANCIS'S LIFE-BOATS AND LIFE-CARS.

BY JACOB ABBOTT.

THE engraving at the head of this article represents the operation of transporting the officers and crew of a wrecked vessel to the shore, by means of one of the Life-Cars invented by Mr. Joseph Francis for this purpose. A considerable appropriation was made recently by Congress, to establish stations along the coast of New Jersey and Long Island—as well as on other parts of the Atlantic seaboard—at which all the apparatus necessary for the service of these cars, and of boats, in cases where boats can be used, may be kept. These stations are maintained by the government, with the aid and co-operation of the Humane Society—a benevolent association the object of which is to provide means for rescuing and saving persons in danger of drowning—and also of the New York Board of Underwriters, a body, which, as its name imports, represents the principal Marine Insurance Companies—associations having a strong pecuniary interest in the saving of cargoes of merchandize, and other property, endangered in a shipwreck. These three parties, the Government, the Humane Society, and the Board of Underwriters, combine their efforts to establish and sustain these stations; though we can not here stop to explain the details of the arrangement by which this co-operation is effected, as we must proceed to consider the more immediate subject of this article, which is the apparatus and the machinery itself, by which

the lives and property are saved. In respect to the stations, however, we will say that it awakens very strong and very peculiar emotions in the mind, to visit one of them on some lonely and desolate coast, remote from human dwellings, and to observe the arrangements and preparations that have been made in them, all quietly awaiting the dreadful emergency which is to call them into action. The traveler stands for example on the southern shore of the island of Nantucket, and after looking off over the boundless ocean which stretches in that direction without limit or shore for thousands of miles, and upon the surf rolling in incessantly on the beach, whose smooth expanse is dotted here and there with the skeleton remains of ships that were lost in former storms, and are now half buried in the sand, he sees, at length, a hut, standing upon the shore just above the reach of the water—the only human structure to be seen. He enters the hut. The surf boat is there, resting upon its rollers, all ready to be launched, and with its oars and all its furniture and appliances complete, and ready for the sea. The fireplace is there, with the wood laid, and matches ready for the kindling. Supplies of food and clothing are also at hand—and a compass: and on a placard, conspicuously posted, are the words,

SHIPWRECKED MARINERS REACHING THIS HUT, IN FOG OR SNOW, WILL FIND THE TOWN OF NANTUCKET TWO MILES DISTANT, DUE WEST.

It is impossible to contemplate such a spectacle as this, without a feeling of strong emotion—and a new and deeper interest in the superior excellency and nobleness of efforts made by man for saving life, and diminishing suffering, in comparison with the deeds of havoc and destruction which have been so much gloried in, in ages that are past. The Life-Boat rests in its retreat, not like a ferocious beast of prey, crouching in its covert to seize and destroy its hapless victims, but like an angel of mercy, reposing upon her wings, and watching for danger, that she may spring forth, on the first warning, to *rescue* and *save*.

The Life-*Car* is a sort of boat, formed of copper or iron, and closed over, above, by a convex deck with a sort of door or hatchway through it, by which the passengers to be con-

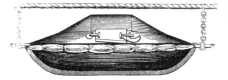

veyed in it to the shore, are admitted. The car will hold from four to five persons. When these passengers are put in, the door, or rather *cover*, is shut down and bolted to its place; and the car is then drawn to the land, suspended by rings from a hawser which has previously been stretched from the ship to the shore.

To be shut up in this manner in so dark and

gloomy a receptacle, for the purpose of being drawn, perhaps at midnight, through a surf of such terrific violence that no boat can live in it, can not be a very agreeable alternative; but the emergencies in which the use of the life-car is called for, are such as do not admit of hesitation or delay. There is no light within the car, and there are no openings for the admission of air.* It is subject, too, in its passage to the shore, to the most frightful shocks and concussions from the force of the breakers. The car, as first made, too, was of such a form as required the passengers within it to lie at length, in a recumbent position, which rendered them almost utterly helpless. The form is, however, now changed—the parts toward the ends, where the heads of the passengers would come, when placed

---

* None such are in fact required, for the car itself contains air enough for the use of its passengers for a quarter of an hour, and there is rarely occupied more than a period of two or three minutes to pass it through the surf to the shore.

in a sitting posture within, being made higher than the middle; and the opening or door is placed in the depressed part, in the centre. This arrangement is found to be much better

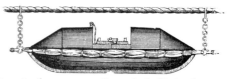

than the former one, as it greatly facilitates the putting in of the passengers, who always require a greater or less degree of aid, and are often entirely insensible and helpless from the effects of fear, or of exposure to cold and hunger. Besides, by this arrangement those who have any strength remaining can take much more convenient and safer positions within the car, in

their progress to the shore, than was possible under the old construction.

The car, as will be seen by the foregoing drawings, is suspended from the hawser by means of short chains attached to the ends of it. These chains terminate in rings above, which rings ride upon the hawser, thus allowing the car to traverse to and fro, from the vessel to the shore. The car is drawn along, in making these passages, by means of lines attached to the two ends of it, one of which passes to the ship and the other to the shore. By means of these lines the empty car is first drawn out to the wreck by the passengers and crew, and then, when loaded, it is drawn back to the land by the people assembled there, as represented in the engraving at the head of this article.

Perhaps the most important and difficult part of the operation of saving the passengers and crew in such cases, is the getting the hawser out in the first instance, so as to form a connection between the ship and the land. In fact, whenever a ship is stranded upon a coast, and people are assembled on the beach to assist the sufferers, the first thing to be done, is always to "get a line ashore." On the success of the attempts made to accomplish this, all the hopes of the sufferers depend. Various methods are resorted to, by the people on board the ship, in order to attain this end, where there are no means at hand on the shore, for effecting it. Perhaps the most common mode is to attach a small line to a cask, or to some other light and bulky substance which the surf can easily throw up upon the shore. The cask, or float, whatever it may be, when attached to the line, is thrown into the water, and after being rolled and tossed, hither and thither, by the tumultuous waves, now advancing, now receding, and now sweeping

THE CASK.

madly around in endless gyrations, it at length reaches a point where some adventurous wrecker on the beach can seize it, and pull it up upon the land. The line is then drawn in, and a hawser being attached to the outer end of it, by the crew of the ship, the end of the hawser itself is then drawn to the shore.

This method, however, of making a communication with the shore from a distressed vessel, simple and sure as it may seem in description, proves generally extremely difficult and uncertain in actual practice. Sometimes, and that, too, not unfrequently when the billows are rolling in with most terrific violence upon the shore, the sea will carry nothing whatever to the land. The surges seem to pass under, and so to get beyond whatever objects lie floating upon the water, so that when a cask is thrown over to them, they play beneath it, leaving it where it was, or even drive it out to sea by not carrying it as far forward on their advance, as they bring it back by their recession. Even the lifeless body of the exhausted mariner, who when his strength was gone and he could cling no longer to the rigging, fell into the sea, is not drawn to the beach, but after surging to and fro for a short period about the vessel, it slowly disappears from view among the foam and the breakers toward the offing. In such cases it is useless to attempt to get a line on shore from the ship by means of any aid from the sea. The cask intrusted with the commission of bearing it, is beaten back against the vessel, or is drifted uselessly along the shore, rolling in and out upon the surges, but never approaching near enough to the beach to enable even the most daring adventurer to reach it.

In case of these life-cars, therefore, arrangements are made for sending the hawser out from the shore to the ship. The apparatus by which this is accomplished consists, first, of a piece of ordnance called a mortar, made large enough to throw a shot of about six inches in diameter; secondly, the shot itself, which has a small iron staple set in it; thirdly, a long line, one end of which is to be attached to the staple in the shot, when the shot is thrown; and, fourthly, a *rack* of a peculiar construction to serve as a reel for winding the line upon. This rack consists of a small square frame, having rows of pegs inserted along the ends and sides of it. The line is wound upon these pegs in such a manner, that as the shot is projected through the air, drawing the line with it, the pegs deliver the line as fast as it is required by the progress of the shot, and that with the least possible friction. Thus the advance of the shot is unimpeded. The mortar from which the shot is fired, is aimed in such a manner as to throw the missile over and beyond the ship, and thus when it falls into the water, the line attached to it comes down across the deck of the ship, and is seized by the passengers and crew.

Sometimes, in consequence of the darkness of the night, the violence of the wind, and perhaps of the agitations and confusion of the scene, the first and even the second trial may not be successful in throwing the line across the wreck. The object is, however, generally attained on the second or third attempt, and then the end of the hawser is drawn out to the wreck by means of the small line which the shot had carried; and being made fast and "drawn taut," the bridge is complete on which the car is to traverse to and fro.

The visitors at Long Branch, a celebrated watering place on the New Jersey coast, near New York, had an opportunity to witness a trial of this apparatus at the station there, during the last summer: a trial made, not in a case of storm and shipwreck, but on a pleasant summer afternoon, and for the purpose of testing

FIRING THE SHOT.

the apparatus, and for practice in the use of it. A large company assembled on the bank to witness the experiments. A boat was stationed on the calm surface of the sea, half a mile from the shore, to represent the wreck. The ball was thrown, the line fell across the boat, the car was drawn out, and then certain amateur performers, representing wrecked and perishing men, were put into the car and drawn safely through the gentle evening surf to the shore.

A case occurred a little more than a year ago on the Jersey shore not very far from Long Branch, in which this apparatus was used in serious earnest. It was in the middle of January and during a severe snow storm. The ship Ayrshire, with about two hundred passengers, had been driven upon the shore by the storm, and lay there stranded, the sea beating over her, and a surf so heavy rolling in, as made it impossible for any boat to reach her. It happened that one of the stations which we have described was near. The people on the shore assembled and brought out the apparatus. They fired the shot, taking aim so well that the line fell directly across the wreck. It was caught by the crew on board and the hawser was hauled off. The car was then attached, and in a short time, every one of the two hundred passengers, men, women, children, and even infants in their mothers' arms, were brought safely through the foaming surges, and landed at the station. The car which performed this service was considered as thenceforth fully entitled to an honorable discharge from active duty, and it now rests, in retirement and repose, though unconscious of its honors, in the Metallic Life-Boat Factory of Mr. Francis, at the Novelty Iron Works.

In many cases of distress and disaster befalling ships on the coast, it is not necessary to use the car, the state of the sea being such that it is possible to go out in a boat, to furnish the necessary succor. The boats, however, which

are destined to this service must be of a peculiar construction, for no ordinary boat can live a moment in the surf which rolls in, in storms, upon shelving or rocky shores. A great many different modes have been adopted for the construction of surf-boats, each liable to its own peculiar objections. The principle on which Mr. Francis relies in his life and surf boats, is to give them an extreme lightness and buoyancy, so as to keep them always upon the *top* of the sea. Formerly it was expected that a boat in such a service, must necessarily take in great quantities of water, and the object of all the contrivances for securing its safety, was to expel the water after it was admitted. In the plan now adopted the design is to exclude the water altogether, by making the structure so light and forming it on such a model that it shall always rise above the wave, and thus glide safely over it. This result is obtained partly by means of the model of the boat, and partly by the lightness of the material of which it is composed. The reader may perhaps be surprised to hear, after this, that the material is *iron*.

Iron—or copper, which in this respect possesses the same properties as iron—though *absolutely* heavier than wood, is, in fact, much lighter as a material for the construction of receptacles of all kinds, on account of its great strength and tenacity, which allows of its being used in plates so thin that the quantity of the material employed is diminished much more than the specific gravity is increased by using the metal. There has been, however, hitherto a great practical difficulty in the way of using iron for such a purpose, namely that of giving to these metal plates a sufficient stiffness. A sheet of tin, for example, though stronger than a board, that is, requiring a greater force to break or rupture it, is still very *flexible*, while the board is stiff. In other words, in the case of a thin plate of metal, the parts yield readily to any *slight* force, so far as to bend under the pressure, but it requires a very great force to separate them entirely; whereas in the case of wood, the slight force is at first resisted, but on a moderate increase of it, the structure breaks down altogether. The great thing to be desired therefore in a material for the construction of boats is to secure the stiffness of wood in conjunction with the thinness and tenacity of iron. This object is attained in the manufacture of Mr. Francis's boats by *plaiting* or *corrugating* the sheets of metal of which the sides of the boat are to be made. A familiar illustration of the principle on which this stiffening is effected is furnished by the common table waiter, which is made, usually, of a thin plate of tinned iron, stiffened by being turned up at the edges all around—the upturned part serving also at the same time the purpose of forming a margin.

The plaitings or corrugations of the metal in these iron boats pass along the sheets, in lines, instead of being, as in the case of the waiter, confined to the margin. The lines which they

form can be seen in the drawing of the surf-boat, given on a subsequent page. The idea of thus corrugating or plaiting the metal was a very simple one; the main difficulty in the invention came, after getting the idea, in devising the ways and means by which such a corrugation could be made. It is a curious circumstance in the history of modern inventions that it often requires much more ingenuity and effort to contrive a way to *make* the article when invented, than it did to invent the article itself. It was, for instance, much easier, doubtless, to invent pins, than to invent the machinery for *making* pins.

The machine for making the corrugations in the sides of these metallic boats consists of a hydraulic press and a set of enormous dies. These dies are grooved to fit each other, and shut together; and the plate of iron which is to be corrugated being placed between them, is pressed into the requisite form, with all the force of the hydraulic piston—the greatest force, altogether, that is ever employed in the service of man.

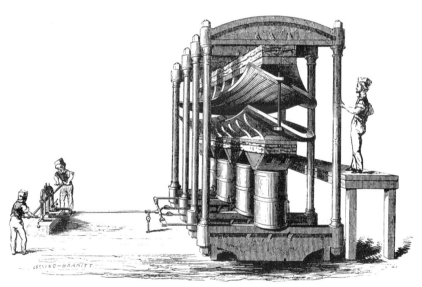

THE HYDRAULIC PRESS.

The machinery referred to will be easily understood by the above engraving. On the left are the pumps, worked, as represented in the engraving, by two men, though four or more are often required. By alternately raising and depressing the break or handle, they work two small but very solid pistons which play within cylinders of corresponding bore, in the manner of any common forcing pump.

By means of these pistons the water is driven, in small quantities but with prodigious force, along through the horizontal tube seen passing across, in the middle of the picture, from the forcing-pump to the great cylinders on the right hand. Here the water presses upward upon the under surfaces of pistons working within the

great cylinders, with a force proportioned to the ratio of the area of those pistons compared with that of one of the pistons in the pump. Now the piston in the force-pump is about one inch in diameter. Those in the great cylinders are about twelve inches in diameter, and as there are four of the great cylinders the ratio is as 1 to 576.* This is a great multiplication, and it is found that the force which the men can exert upon the piston within the small cylinder, by the aid of the long lever with which they work it, is so great, that when multiplied by 576, as it is by being expanded over the

---

* Areas being as the squares of homologous lines, the ratio would be, mathematically expressed, $1^2 : 4 \times 12^2 = 1 : 4 \times 144 = 1 : 576$.

surface of the large pistons, an upward pressure results of about eight hundred tons. This is a force ten times as great in *intensity* as that exerted by steam in the most powerful sea-going engines. It would be sufficient to lift a block of granite five or six feet square at the base, and as high as the Bunker Hill Monument.

Superior, however, as this force is, in one point of view, to that of steam, it is very inferior to it in other respects. It is great, so to speak, in *intensity*, but it is very small in *extent* and *amount*. It is capable indeed of lifting a very great weight, but it can raise it only an exceedingly little way. Were the force of such an engine to be brought into action beneath such a block of granite as we have described, the enormous burden would rise, but it would rise by a motion almost inconceivably slow, and after going up perhaps as high as the thickness of a sheet of paper, the force would be spent, and no further effect would be produced without a new exertion of the motive power. In other words, the whole amount of the force of a hydraulic engine, vastly concentrated as it is, and irresistible, within the narrow limits within which it works, is but the force of four or five men after all; while the power of the engines of a Collins' steamer is equal to that of four or five thousand men. The steam-engine can do an *abundance* of *great* work; while, on the other hand, what the hydraulic press can do is very little in *amount*, and only great in view of its extremely concentrated intensity.

Hydraulic presses are consequently very often used, in such cases and for such purposes as require a great force within very narrow limits. The indentations made by the type in printing the pages of this magazine, are taken out, and the sheet rendered smooth again, by hydraulic presses exerting a force of *twelve* hundred tons. This would make it necessary for us to carry up our imaginary block of granite *a hundred feet higher* than the Bunker Hill Monument to get a load for them.*

In Mr. Francis's presses, the dies between which the sheets of iron or copper are pressed, are directly above the four cylinders which we have described, as will be seen by referring once more to the drawing. The upper die is fixed—being firmly attached to the top of the frame, and held securely down by the rows of iron pillars on the two sides, and by the massive iron caps, called platens, which may be seen passing across at the top, from pillar to pillar. These caps are held by large iron nuts which are screwed down over the ends of the pillars above. The lower die is movable. It is attached by massive iron work to the ends of the

* There are nine of these presses in the printing-rooms of Harper and Brothers, all constantly employed in smoothing sheets of paper after the printing. The sheets of paper to be pressed are placed between sheets of very smooth and thin, but *hard* pasteboard, until a pile is made several feet high, and containing sometimes two thousand sheets of paper, and then the hydraulic pressure is applied. These presses cost, each, from twelve to fifteen hundred dollars.

piston-rods, and of course it rises when the pistons are driven upward by the pressure of the water. The plate of metal, when the dies approach each other, is bent and drawn into the intended shape by the force of the pressure, receiving not only the corrugations which are designed to stiffen it, but also the general shaping necessary, in respect to swell and curvature, to give it the proper form for the side, or the portion of a side, of a boat.

It is obviously necessary that these dies should fit each other in a very accurate manner, so as to compress the iron equally in every part. To make them fit thus exactly, massive as they are in magnitude, and irregular in form, is a work of immense labor. They are first cast as nearly as possible to the form intended, but as such castings always warp more or less in cooling, there is a great deal of fitting afterward required, to make them come rightly together. This could easily be done by machinery if the surfaces were square, or cylindrical, or of any other mathematical form to which the working of machinery could be adapted. But the curved and winding surfaces which form the hull of a boat or vessel, smooth and flowing as they are, and controlled, too, by established and well-known laws, bid defiance to all the attempts of mere mechanical motion to follow them. The superfluous iron, therefore, of these dies, must all be cut away by chisels driven by a hammer held in the hand; and so great is the labor required to fit and smooth and polish them, that a pair of them costs several thousand dollars before they are completed and ready to fulfill their function.

The superiority of metallic boats, whether of copper or iron, made in the manner above described, over those of any other construction, is growing every year more and more apparent. They are more light and more easily managed, they require far less repair from year to year, and are very much longer lived. When iron is used for this purpose, a preparation is employed that is called *galvanized* iron. This manufacture consists of plates of iron of the requisite thickness, coated on each side, first with tin, and then with zinc; the tin being used simply as a solder, to unite the other metals. The plate presents, therefore, to the water, only a surface of *zinc*, which resists all action, so that the boats thus made are subject to no species of decay. They can be injured or destroyed only by violence, and even violence acts at a very great disadvantage in attacking them. The stroke of a shot, or a concussion of any kind that would split or shiver a wooden boat so as to damage it past repair, would only indent, or at most perforate, an iron one. And a perforation even, when made, is very easily repaired, even by the navigators themselves, under circumstances however unfavorable. With a smooth and heavy stone placed upon the outside for an anvil, and another used on the inside as a hammer, the protrusion is easily beaten down, the opening is closed, the continuity of

WRECKED AND WRECKERS

EARLY HOUSE OF REFUGE AND LOOK-OUT STATION.

surface is restored, and the damaged boat becomes, excepting, perhaps, in the imagination of the navigator, as good once more as ever.

Metallic boats of this character were employed by the party under Lieut. Lynch, in making, some years ago, their celebrated voyage down the river Jordan to the Dead Sea. The navigation of this stream was difficult and perilous in the highest degree. The boats were subject to the severest possible tests and trials. They were impelled against rocks, they were dragged over shoals, they were swept down cataracts and cascades. There was one *wooden* boat in the little squadron; but this was soon so strained and battered that it could no longer be kept afloat, and it was abandoned. The metallic boats, however, lived through the whole, and finally floated in peace on the heavy waters of the Dead Sea, in nearly as good a condition as when they first came from Mr. Francis's dies.

The seams of a metallic boat will never open by exposure to the sun and rain, when lying long upon the deck of a ship, or hauled up upon a shore. Nor will such boats burn. If a ship takes fire at sea, the boats, if of iron, can never be injured by the conflagration. Nor can they be sunk. For they are provided with air chambers in various parts, each separate from the others, so that if the boat were bruised and jammed by violent concussions, up to her utmost capacity of receiving injury, the shapeless mass would still float upon the sea, and hold up with unconquerable buoyancy as many as could cling to her.*

A curious instance occurred during the late war with Mexico which illustrates the almost indestructible character of these metallic boats. The reader is probably aware that the city of Vera Cruz is situated upon a low and sandy coast, and that the only port which exists there is formed by a small island which lies at a little distance from the shore, and a mole or pier built out from it into the water. The island is almost wholly covered by the celebrated fortress of St. Juan de Ulloa. Ships obtain something like shelter under the lee of this island and mole, riding sometimes at anchor behind the mole, and sometimes moored to iron rings set in the castle walls. At one time while the American forces were in possession of the city, an officer of the army had occasion to use a boat for some purpose of transportation from the island to the shore. He applied to the naval authorities in order to procure one. He was informed that there was no boat on the station that could be spared for such a purpose. In this dilemma the officer accidentally learned that there was an old copper life-boat, lying in the water near the castle landing, dismantled, sunk, and useless. The officer resolved, as a last resort, to examine this wreck, in hopes to find that it might possibly be raised and repaired.

He found that the boat was lying in the water and half filled with rocks, sand, and masses of old iron, which had been thrown into her to sink and destroy her. Among the masses of iron there was a heavy bar which had been used apparently in the attempt to punch holes in the boat by those who had undertaken to sink her. These attempts had been generally fruitless, the blows having only made indentations in the copper, on account of the yielding nature of the metal. In one place, however, in the bottom of the boat, the work had been done effectually; for five large holes were discovered there, at a place where the bottom of the boat rested upon the rocks so as to furnish such points of resistance below as prevented the copper from yielding to the blows.

The officer set his men at work to attempt to repair this damage. They first took out the sand and stones and iron with which the boat was encumbered, and then raising her, they dragged her up out of the water to the landing. Here the men lifted her up upon her side, and began to beat back the indentations which had been made in the metal, by holding a heavy sledge hammer on the inside, to serve as an anvil, and then striking with a hand-hammer upon the protuberances on the outside. In the same manner they beat back the burrs or protrusions formed where the holes had been punched through the bottom of the boat, and they found, much to their satisfaction, that when the metal was thus brought back into its place the holes were closed again, and the boat became whole and tight as before.

When this work was done the men put the boat back again in her proper position, replaced and fastened the seats, and then launched her into the water. They found her stanch and tight, and seemingly as good as new. The whole work of repairing her did not occupy more than one hour—much less time, the officer thought, than had been spent in the attempt to destroy her.

The boat thus restored was immediately put to service and she performed the work required of her, admirably well. She was often out on the open sea in very rough weather, but always rode over the billows in safety, and in the end proved to be the strongest, swiftest, and safest boat in the gulf squadron.

The *surf*-boats, made in this way, will ride safely in any sea—and though sometimes after protracted storms, the surges roll in upon shelving or rocky shores with such terrific violence that it is impossible to get the boats off from the land, yet once off, they are safe, however wild the commotion. In fact there is a certain charm in the graceful and life-like buoyancy

---

* The principle on which these life-boats are made is found equally advantageous in its application to boats intended for other purposes. For a gentleman's pleasure-grounds, for example, how great the convenience of having a boat which is always stanch and tight—which no exposure to the sun can make leaky, which no wet can rot, and no neglect impair. And so in all other cases where boats are required for situations or used where they will be exposed to hard usage of any kind, whether from natural causes or the neglect or inattention of those in charge of them, this material seems far superior to any other.

THE SURF-BOAT.

with which they ride over the billows, and in the confidence and sense of security which they inspire in the hearts of those whom they bear, as they go bounding over the crests of the waves, that it awakens in minds of a certain class, a high exhilaration and pleasure, to go out in them upon stormy and tempestuous seas. To illustrate the nature of the scenes through which such adventurers sometimes pass, we will close this article with a narrative of a particular excursion made not long since by one of these boats—a narrative now for the first time reduced to writing.

One dark and stormy night Mr. Richard C. Holmes, the collector at the port of Cape May, a port situated on an exposed and dangerous part of the coast, near the entrance to the Chesapeake, was awakened from his sleep by the violence of the storm, and listening, he thought that he could hear at intervals the distant booming of a gun, which he supposed to be a signal of distress. He arose and hastened to the shore. The night was dark, and nothing could be seen but the report of the gun was distinctly to be heard, at brief intervals, coming apparently from a great distance in the offing.

He aroused from the neighboring houses a sufficient number of other persons to man his surf-boat, embarked on board, taking a compass for a guide, and put to sea.

It was very dark and the weather was very thick, so that nothing could be seen; but the crew of the boat pulled steadily on, guided only by the compass, and by the low and distant booming of the gun. They rowed in the direction of the sound, listening as they pulled; but the noise made by the winds and the waves, and by the dashing of the water upon the boat and upon the oars, was so loud and incessant, and the progress which they made against the heavy "send" of the surges was so slow, that it was for a long time doubtful whether they were advancing or not. After an hour or two, however, the sound of the gun seemed to come nearer, and at length they could see, faintly, the flash

beaming out for an instant just before the report, in the midst of the driving rain and flying spray which filled the dark air before them.

Encouraged by this, the oarsmen pulled at their oars with new energy, and soon came in sight of the hull of the distressed vessel, which began now to rise before them, a black and misshapen mass, scarcely distinguishable from the surrounding darkness and gloom. As they came nearer, they found that the vessel was a ship—that she had been beaten down upon her side by the sea, and was almost overwhelmed with the surges which were breaking over her. Every place upon the deck which afforded any possibility of shelter was crowded with men and women, all clinging to such supports as were within their reach, and vainly endeavoring to screen themselves from the dashing of the spray. The boat was to the leeward of the vessel, but so great was the commotion of the sea, that it was not safe to approach even near enough to communicate with the people on board. After coming up among the heaving and tumbling surges as near as they dared to venture, the crew of the surf boat found that all attempts to make their voices heard were unavailing, as their loudest shouts were wholly overpowered by the roaring of the sea, and the howling of the winds in the rigging.

Mr. Holmes accordingly gave up the attempt, and fell back again, intending to go round to the windward side of the ship, in hopes to be able to communicate with the crew from that quarter. He could hear *them* while he was to leeward of them, but they could not hear him; and his object in wishing to communicate with them was to give them directions in respect to what they were to do, in order to enable him to get on board.

In the mean time daylight began to appear. The position of the ship could be seen more distinctly. She lay upon a shoal, held partly by her anchor, which the crew had let go before she struck. Thus confined she had been knocked down by the seas, and now lay thumping vio-

42

lently at every rising and falling of the surge, and in danger every moment of going to pieces. She was covered with human beings, who were seen clinging to her in every part—each separate group forming a separate and frightful spectacle of distress and terror.

Mr. Holmes succeeded in bringing the surf-boat so near to the ship on the windward side as to hail the crew, and he directed them to let down a line from the end of the main yard, to leeward. The main yard is a spar which lies horizontally at the head of the main mast, and as the vessel was careened over to leeward, the end of the yard on that side would of course be depressed, and a line from it would hang down over the water, entirely clear of the vessel. The crew heard this order and let down the line. Mr. Holmes then ordered the surf-boat to be pulled away from the ship again, intending to drop to leeward once more, and there to get on board of it by means of the line. In doing this, however, the boat was assailed by the winds and waves with greater fury than ever, as if

they now first began to understand that it had come to rescue their victims from their power. The boat was swept so far away by this onset, that it was an hour before the oarsmen could get her back so as to approach the line. It seemed then extremely dangerous to approach it, as the end of it was flying hither and thither, whipping the surges which boiled beneath it, or whirling and curling in the air, as it was swung to and fro by the impulse of the wind, or by the swaying of the yard-arm from which it was suspended.

The boat however approached the line. Mr. Holmes, when he saw it within reach, sprang forward to the bows, and after a moment's contest between an instinctive shrinking from the gigantic lash which was brandished so furiously over his head, and his efforts to reach it, he at length succeeded in seizing it. He grasped it by both hands with all his force, and the next instant the boat was swept away from beneath him by the retreating billows, and he was left safely dangling in the air.

CLIMBING THE ROPE.

We say *safely*, for, whenever any one of these indomitable sea-kings, no matter in what circumstances of difficulty or danger, gets a rope that is well secured at its point of suspension, fairly within his iron gripe, we may at once dismiss all concern about his personal safety. In this case the intrepid adventurer, when he found that the boat had surged away from beneath him, and left him suspended in the air over the raging and foaming billows, felt that all danger was over. To mount the rope, hand over hand, till he gained the yard-arm, to clamber up the yard to the mast, and then to descend to the deck by the shrouds, required only an *ordinary* exercise of nautical strength and courage. All this was done in a moment, and Mr. Holmes stood upon the deck, speechless, and entirely overcome by the appalling spectacle of terror and distress that met his view.

The crew gathered around the stranger, whom they looked upon at once as their deliverer, and listened to hear what he had to say. He informed them that the ship was grounded on a narrow reef or bar running parallel with the coast, and that there was deeper water between them and the shore. He counseled them to cut loose from the anchor, in which case he presumed that the shocks of the seas would drive the ship over the bar, and that then she would drift rapidly in upon the shore; where, when she should strike upon the beach, they could probably find means to get the passengers to the land.

This plan was decided upon. The cable was cut away by means of such instruments as came to hand. The ship was beaten over the bar, awakening, as she was dashed along, new shrieks from the terrified passengers, at the violence of the concussions. Once in deep water she moved on more smoothly, but was still driven at a fearful rate directly toward the land. The surf-boat accompanied her, hovering as near to her all the way as was consistent with safety. During their progress the boat was watched by the passengers on board the ship, with anxious eyes, as in her were centred all their hopes of escape from destruction.

The conformation of this part of the coast, as in many other places along the shores of the United States, presents a range of low, sandy islands, lying at a little distance from the land, and separated from it by a channel of sheltered water. These islands are long and narrow, and separated from each other by inlets or openings here and there, formed apparently by the breaking through of the sea. The crew of our ship would have been glad to have seen some possibility of their entering through one of these inlets. The ship could not, however, be guided, but must go wherever the winds and waves chose to impel her. This was to the outer shore of one of the long, narrow islands, where at length she struck again, and was again overwhelmed with breakers and spray.

After much difficulty the seamen succeeded, with the help of the surf-boat, in getting a line from the ship to the shore, by means of which one party on the land and another on board the vessel could draw the surf-boat to and fro. In this way the passengers and crew were all safely landed. When the lives were thus all safe, sails and spars were brought on shore, and then, under Mr. Holmes's directions, a great tent was constructed on the sand, which, though rude in form, was sufficient in size to shelter all the company. When all were assembled the num-

THE TENT.

ber of passengers saved was found to be *one hundred and twenty-one.* They were German emigrants of the better class, and they gathered around their intrepid deliverer, when all was over, with such overwhelming manifestations of their admiration and gratitude, as wholly unmanned him. They had saved money, and jewels, and such other valuables as could be carried about the person, to a large amount; and they brought every thing to him, pressing him most earnestly, and with many tears, to take it all, for having saved them from such imminent and certain destruction. He was deeply moved by these expressions of gratitude, but he would receive no reward.

When the tent was completed and the whole company were comfortably established under the shelter of it, the boat was passed to and fro again through the surf, to bring provisions on shore. A party of seamen remained on board for this purpose—loading the boat at the ship, and drawing it out again when unloaded on the shore. The company that were assembled under the tent dried their clothes by fires built for the purpose there, and then made a rude breakfast from the provisions brought for them from the ship: and when thus in some degree rested and refreshed, they were all conveyed safely in boats to the main land.

WRECK OF THE "CATHARINE."

RESCUE.

"THEY FOUND HIM NEARLY DEAD."

...One of the most gallant and skillful crews in the service was lost at Point aux Barques, Lake Huron, in October, 1880, and the heart-rending details of the calamity are known to the world through its sole survivor. These loyal men went out in the surf-boat in prompt response to a signal of distress displayed upon a vessel three miles away. The boat was capsized and righted several times, but finally remained capsized, the men clinging to it; but the cold was such that one after another perished, until six were gone. The keeper drifted upon the beach, insensible, and was found steadying himself by the trunk of a tree...He was so much injured that he resigned his position; thus the station was in one day bereft of its entire crew. These heroic men had during the same year saved nearly a hundred lives.

Harper's Monthly, February 1882.

THE SHIPWRECK AT NIGHT.

Upon the Atlantic coast, much more frequently than elsewhere, the sea is too heavy in a winter storm for the use of the boat, and resort is had, as has been seen, to the life-saving ordnance. The process of throwing a temporary suspension-bridge from the land to the wreck, first suggested by Lieutenant Bell, of the royal artillery, in 1791, and matured and carried into practical effect by Captain Manby, of the royal navy, has been greatly improved during the last few years. The first gun in use was of

cast iron, weighing two hundred and eighty-eight pounds, and throwing a spherical ball with line attached, its extreme range being four hundred and twenty-one yards. This gave place to the Parrott gun, weighing two hundred and sixty-six pounds – a slight gain – with a maximum range of four hundred and seventy-three yards. The first ball fired in the United States to save life is preserved in the museum of the Life-saving Service with tender care. It was at the wreck of the *Ayrshire*, on Squan Beach, New Jersey, in 1850, and two hundred and one lives were saved by its means. The Lyle gun, of bronze, weighing one hundred and eighty-five pounds, with a range of six hundred and ninety-five yards, or nearly half a mile, has recently superseded all others, and is universally conceded to be the best in existence. It was the result of experiments in 1878, Lieutenant D.A. Lyle, of the Ordnance Department at Springfield, Massachusetts, having been detailed, by request of the superintendent of the Service, to assist Captain Merryman in solving the problem of the extension of the shot-line and a reduction in the weight of the gun. The projectile has a shank protruding four inches from the muzzle, to an eye in which the shot-line is tied – a device which prevents it from being burned off by the ignited gases in firing. The rocket, so much used abroad, is uncertain, and the line is apt to break at its attachment to the shot, or become badly twisted on its way. The shot-line in use, like the gun, is the result of a series of careful experiments. It is made of unbleached linen thread, very closely and smoothly braided, and water-proofed. It is coiled into a faking box with such precision that it will pay out freely, and fly to a wreck without entanglement or friction. The projectile must be aimed so that the line falls over the ship – not an easy mark to hit in the night in the midst of a blinding storm; and in case of failure, the line is quickly drawn in, and French-faked, that is, laid out in loops upon a tarpaulin spread upon the beach, ready for the second shot. The sailors, as soon as it reaches them, pull upon it until the whip or hauling-line (an inch and a half in circumference), which is made fast to the shore end of the shot-line, is drawn on board with a pulley-block, or tail-block, and a tablet, or tally-board, with instructions how to arrange it for use. When this is fixed, the surfmen haul upon part of the whip, and send the hawser, which rests on a crotch quickly erected on shore as a sort of temporary pier. The sand-anchor sustains this slender bridge of rope. It is two pieces of wood crossed on their centres and bolted together, and is buried in a trench behind the crotch, and connected with the hawser by a double pulley-block. The breeches-buoy is drawn to and fro upon these ropes, bringing one person at a time. All this seems very easy on paper, particularly when the sun shines through the lattice, or the reader occupies a soft-cushioned chair before a warm, cheerful fire. But when darkness reigns, and the winds howl, and every drop of spray freezes until the rescuers are incased in ice, and the wreck rises and rolls and turns half-somersaults with each gust, in total disregard of the convenience of the surfmen, and a hundred possible mishaps lurk just beyond the borders of vision, the aspect changes, and the reality becomes more wonderful than any trick of fancy or fiction.

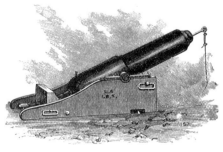

THE LYLE GUN.

"THE SHATTER OF THE SEA."

WRECK OF THE "HURON."

LIFE-BOAT STATION ON LAKE MICHIGAN.

SELF-RIGHTING LIFE-BOAT.

A RESCUE.

WORKING A PRIMITIVE BREECHES-BUOY THROUGH THE SURF

THE LIFEBOAT TAKING SAILORS FROM A WRECK

THE WRECK.

FOR A LIST OF BOOKS on other topics of American history—Pony Express, Overland Emigration, Custer's Last Battle, John Muir, Theodore Roosevelt, Donner Party, Discovery of Yosemite, Yellowstone/Grand Teton, Bodie, Hawaii, Arkansas Hot Springs, Indian Rock Art, Mark Twain, Famous Gunfighters, and more—write the address below:

VISTABOOKS
2487 Industrial Blvd #2
Grand Junction, CO 81505